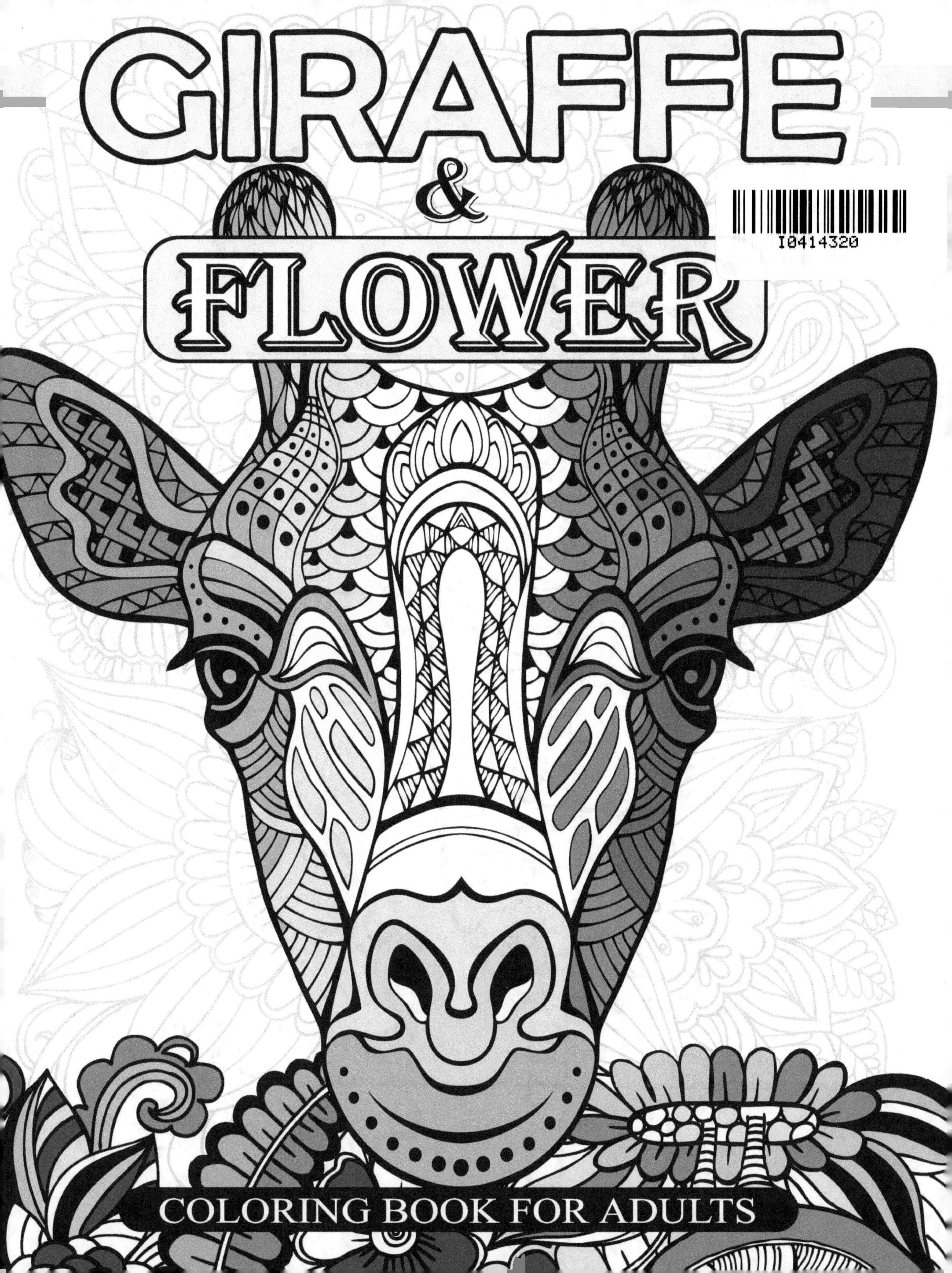
GIRAFFE
&
FLOWER
I0414320
COLORING BOOK FOR ADULTS

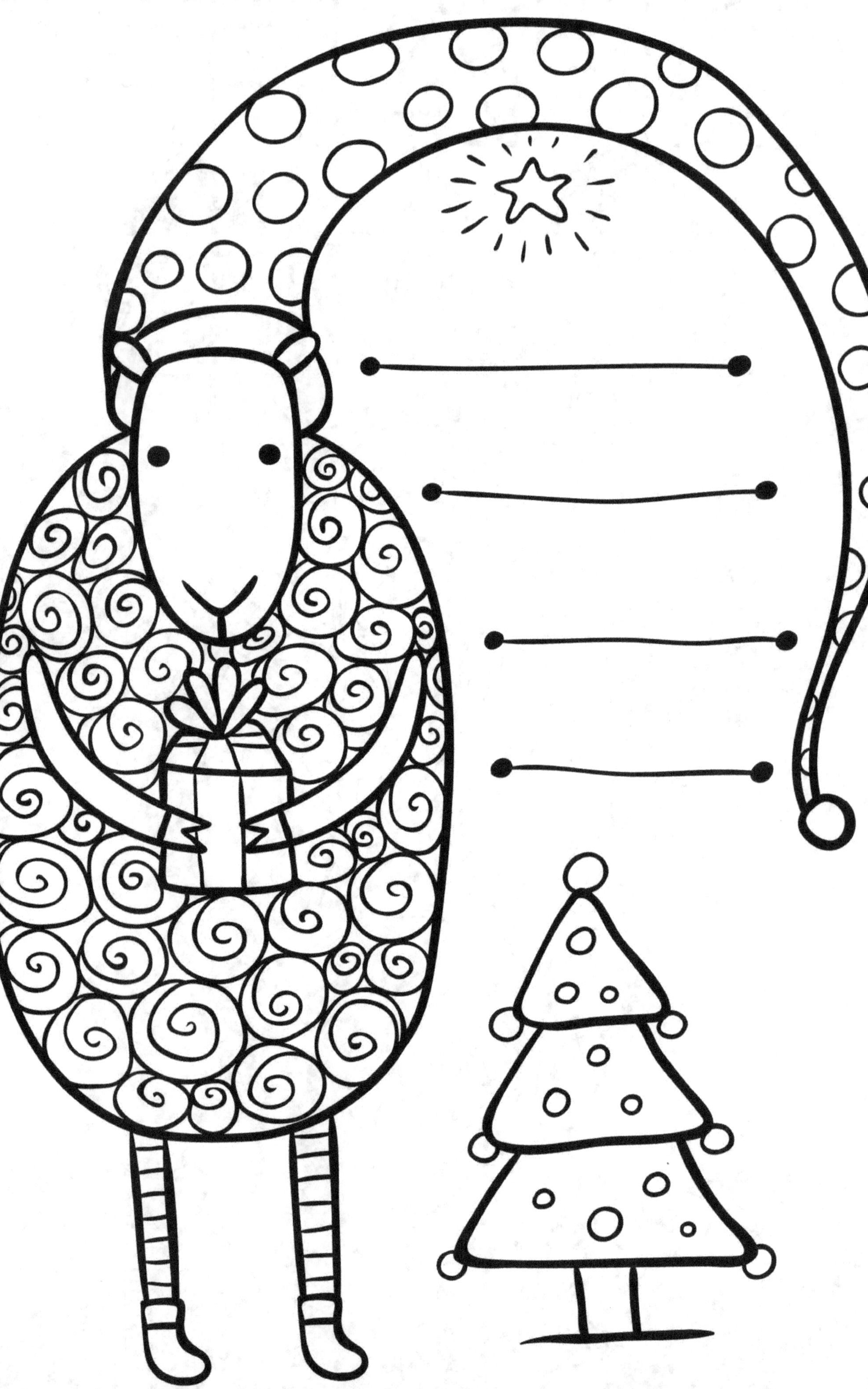

free download coloring pages

At : bit.ly/get_sample_free

www.ingramcontent.com/pod-product-compliance
Lightning Source LLC
Chambersburg PA
CBHW081155280526
45787CB00008B/3336
* 9 7 8 1 5 4 6 8 7 5 8 5 7 *